AMBROSE

by Mac Conner

Order this book online at www.trafford.com
or email orders@trafford.com

Most Trafford titles are also available at major online book retailers.

© Copyright 2011 Mac Conner.

All rights reserved. No part of this publication may be reproduced, stored in a retrieval system, or transmitted, in any form or by any means, electronic, mechanical, photocopying, recording, or otherwise, without the written prior permission of the author.

Printed in the United States of America.

ISBN: 978-1-4269-6578-4

Library of Congress Control Number: 2011906121

Trafford rev. 06/14/2011

 www.trafford.com

North America & international
toll-free: 1 888 232 4444 (USA & Canada)
phone: 250 383 6864 • fax: 812 355 4082

AMBROSE
by Mac Conner

Ambrose was the name that was given to him by the neighborhood gang. No one seemed to know why he was given that name, but it seemed to fit him.

I suppose, before I write any further I ought to explain that Ambrose was a pig, but he wasn't just an ordinary pig, he was a runt. A runt is one of those unfortunate whose mother isn't able to accommodate it because there are too many to manage in the family.

The first time I saw Ambrose he was very small and looked awfully hungry. The farmer, who owned him, told us boys that Ambrose would probably die if someone didn't take care of him, and feed him with a nipple and bottle.

Naturally we all wanted to take him home with us. After arguing for awhile we decided to flip a coin, and I was the lucky one.

I was pretty happy about the whole affair until I got him home and my mother told me to take Ambrose right back to where I got him. After the usual amount of pleading and crying, I persuaded her to let me keep him for a week or two at the least.

After a week or so everyone had become so attached to him that we decided to keep him for a little while longer. He seemed to like us too, but I think his best friend was our dog. They were inseparable friends.

If the dog went out to chase rabbits, Ambrose went along and seemed to enjoy it as much as the dog did. Some people actually said that if Ambrose could have run faster he would been a better rabbit dog, then the dog itself.

Ambrose probably holds the record for having his name in the paper more than any other pig, even if it was in the lost and found column. The reason for this was because he would follow the dog around town and get lost.

One day it was decided that Ambrose was getting too big to be running around loose, and so it was decided to sell him.

The man, who bought him, put him in pig pen with some other pigs. If it is possible for a pig to look as if his pride were hurt, then Ambrose most certainly had that look.

He had never been near another pig except when he was first born, and so he didn't know what they were. He refused to eat with them so the owner decided to put him in a separate pen so the children can visit him.

Although, I don't know just what Ambrose thought he was, I bet he died, thankful, that he wasn't just an ordinary pig.

Illustrator: Alice Cleveland

www.ingramcontent.com/pod-product-compliance
Lightning Source LLC
Chambersburg PA
CBHW041543040426
42446CB00002B/210